The Art of
LEADING

The Art of
LEADING

3 Principles for Predictable
Performance Improvement

Wally Hauck

The Art of Leading

GRATITUDE

I want to thank my wife Lorraine who was so supportive and provided frequent and sometimes emotional reviews of my work. I especially thank my two daughters Emily and Erin who have inspired me to be the very best father I can be and have taught me that being a good father requires many of the same characteristics of being a good leader.

I also want to thank all of my wonderful customers who have played a very active role to help me clarify and codify the principles over the past 15 years. These include, but are not limited to, Sergio Huerta, Barbara McCleary, David McQuaide, Merrilyn Ramsey, Joseph Whaley, Mark Crane, Margaret Zimmerman, Kathy Knowles, Dave Rankin, Mel Palmer, Ben Pressly, Joseph Hickey, Lisa Blunt-Bradley, Jack Markell, Dana Jefferson, Cindy Fauerbach, Tricia Neeley, Ann Visali, Dianne Auger, Lisa Marks, Gregg Barratt, Julia Groom-Thompson, Jim Hamilton, Bruce and Eliane Pauley, Robert D'Andrea, Jennifer Segal, Robert Heath, Henry Mustacato, Mauva Carasco, Hugh McCann, Tim McCann, Sarah McCann, Kathy Saint, Beth Abarca, Doug Hovey, Jim Kimple, Keith Kleps, Eleanor Arno, Lisa Delohery, Robert Martinez, Bob Agnew, Sal Olivas, Anita Gliniecki, Martin Schwartz, Virginia Cueto, Peggy Baker, Marshall Thurber, Karl Haushaulter, William Worcester, Katie Banzhaf, Sandra Anderson-Howell, Merle Berke-Schlessel, David Kennedy, Marjolijn Wijsenbeek, Brenda Liebers-Moore, Jeffery Stoyer. Special thanks to Don Espach and Brandon Yusuf Toropov for being so encouraging and helpful in the production of this book.

Finally, my good friends and colleagues at the National Speakers Association both in Connecticut and across the country have been, and continue to be, an incredible resource.

TABLE OF CONTENTS

Introduction

"Leadership is much more an art, a belief, a condition of the heart, than a set of things to do. The visible signs of artful leadership are expressed, ultimately, in its practice." —Max Depree

An artist is open to completely new ways of thinking about problems. He/she brings creativity and insight to life and to work instead of choosing to be obedient to existing common approaches to persistent problems. You can be an artist in your leadership activities. You can open new possibilities by adopting new ways of thinking. You can bring the art of leading to life.

"I do not judge success based on championships; rather, I judge it on how close we came to realizing our potential." – John Wooden

Bill Walsh, the renowned National Football League coach, had an unusual belief about quarterbacks: *"They are only as good as the system they play in."*

In 1970-71, while an offensive coordinator for the Cincinnati Bengals, Walsh developed a passing game system for Virgil Carter, a below-average quarterback who had never even completed half of his passes in a full season. That new system propelled Carter to lead the National Football League in completion percentage at 62.2%; the system also increased his yards per completion by 24% (increasing from 5.9 to 7.3).

In 1979, Walsh joined the San Francisco 49ers as head coach. He used the same system he had employed in Cincinnati to propel another quarterback, Steve Deberg (who by most statistical measures was one of the NFL's worst passers) from a 45.4% completion rate to an astonishing 60%. That year, Deberg ended up throwing more completions than any other quarterback in NFL history up to that point.

In the two years that followed, Walsh found Joe Montana who is now known in many circles as the "best quarterback" in NFL history. I prefer to think that all three quarterbacks took advantage of the best *system* in NFL history – a system that challenged them, successfully, to reach their full potential.

How did Walsh do it? He didn't try to change the quarterback. Instead, he changed the system within which the quarterbacks played.

This is a book about changing the system – rather than trying to change the person. Its central tenet is *"A player is only as good as system he or she plays in."* This core belief flies in the face of the typical belief held by the typical organizational culture, which, whether stated explicitly or not, usually holds that the individual's performance can be measured and improved separately from the system within which he or she works. This is false!

Now more than ever, this type of thinking must be challenged vigorously wherever it appears. Our economy is now "brain based" rather than "labor based." While few managers would dispute that we are living in "the Information Age," many companies are still employing management tools developed during the various phases of the Industrial Revolution, the era when machine-driven economies were the rule. The need to make the shift in thinking to Information Age management has never been greater.

The very complexity of the new competitive world requires a new kind of leadership, one that anticipates both continuous information exchange among the organization's units, and the need to understand and adapt more quickly to trends and techniques that might be taking place half a world away.

Today's managers must assimilate an enormous amount of information. Successful leaders must increasingly seek more efficient ways to access timely, complete and accurate data. Without the latest technology, competitive advantage will suffer. What many managers fail to realize is that this principle applies to the management of people, as it does to every other aspect of business. Consider this book part of the "technology" you can use to establish a competitive edge in your industry. It's an upgrade for leadership skills and is as essential as an operating system upgrade to run the latest computer software.

THE EINSTEIN CHALLENGE

CEOs want positive results – but they often see many of the problems they have sworn to resolve repeat themselves persistently. Einstein once said, "We can't solve problems by using the same kind of thinking we used when we created them." If our problems repeat, we must change our thinking if we want to dissolve them and prevent them from recurring. Unless we upgrade our thinking, and do so in a way that improves the level of commitment our employees have to our organization, we can expect the same problems to repeat themselves in an endless cycle.

WE NEED AN UPGRADE IN LEADERSHIP – HERE IS PROOF!

According to WorkUSA® 2002, a Watson and Wyatt Study of Employee Attitudes and Opinions, only:

- 39% of employees at U.S. companies trust the senior leaders at their firms.
- 31% of employees rate their companies as "effective" with regard to internal communication.
- 52% of employees understand how their jobs connect with the company strategy.
- 25% of employees say their companies reward people effectively for their contributions.

According to the Gallup Organization:

- It costs at least 100% to 150% of the employee's salary to replace him/her.
- There are three basic reasons why employees leave their jobs:
  1. Mis-hiring – poor hiring process and poor orientation or training

2. Lack of growth opportunities – unclear career path

3. Poor relationship with the boss, who is often seen as too controlling or too distant

- Only 26% of employees can be considered to be committed. "Committed" means the employee is: sincerely passionate, fully focused, challenged, innovative, solves problems voluntarily, productive, proud, does high quality work, willing to volunteers to do more when necessary, likely to offer to help to others without being asked.

  * Roughly 75% are either non-committed or disruptive. However, 91% of committed employees intend to be with the company for at least the next 12 months.

- Companies with high levels of employee commitment have nearly six times the margin of those whose employees have low commitment.

According to a study by Leadership IQ (August 2007):

- 93% of people have avoided confronting a coworker about inappropriate behavior, even when a customer or the organization suffered as a result.

- 81% of managers have avoided confronting a subordinate about inappropriate behavior, even when a customer or the organization suffered as a result.

- 89% of people have avoided confronting their boss when he or she failed to fulfill an expectation or promise.

- One analysis revealed that 37% of an employee's willingness to stay at his or her company is driven by the person's comfort level with speaking the truth about these sensitive issues.
- 77% of respondents say that, when they speak up about sensitive topics, the other party gets angry or defensive.
- 83% of respondents say that they occasionally or frequently withhold important information from bosses, coworkers and employees because they fear the conversation will end badly.

These kinds of results prove that we have serious problems with team building, engagement, and performance in our workplaces.

If we have problems, we must decide how to solve them. This book offers a way of thinking and a set of strategies that leaders can implement in their organizations to accelerate results and break the cycle of repeating problems. The problems are chronic *because our way of thinking must change.*

WHO IS THIS BOOK FOR?

This book is for any leader who:

- Has direct reports
- Is new to his/her job and wants to start out on the right leadership foot
- Is frustrated by the current performance review process
- Wants significant employee engagement as a competitive edge

- Is frustrated with the status-quo
- Has always had a nagging sense that the typical management books are flawed
- Has people problems and is frustrated with current solutions
- Is not afraid to try something new
- Wants to take the long term view
- Cares about people
- Cares about customers

Are you disappointed with the behaviors of some employees? Do employees who report to you complain about unfair distribution of work? Are you frustrated by the current performance appraisal process? Do you enter appraisal *meetings with* anxiety or trepidation? Are you concerned they actually make things worse? Are you disappointed with the speed of improvement within the organization or with individuals? Are you concerned about the level of trust and relationships between management and employees? Are you disappointed in the quality of customer service?

These are all symptoms of a work culture that needs an upgrade. Fortunately, you can channel these concerns and emotions into the motivation to make a change. If you have influence over processes, policies, and procedures you will find ideas here to make constructive changes. If you have control over the decisions about how performance appraisals are conducted in your organization, you can use the tools outlined in this book to significantly improve the performance of your team. However, even if you have only limited control, because those decisions are made at a higher level, you can still benefit by implementing ideas from this book that *are* under your control, such as how to approach the meeting, how you talk to your employees and even how to influence and speak with your own boss.

If you are the leader of the organization, I recommend you implement every single action step in this book. If you are not the leader but you are a manager with people on your team reporting to you, I recommend you implement as many of the action steps as you can. Even if you are an employee with no direct reports, you will still find this book useful, because it will help you to identify the action steps you want your manager to implement; at a time that makes sense to you, you can ask him/her to cooperate and try those action steps as an experiment.

WHY LEADERSHIP IS SO CHALLENGING (A PARADOX)

Let's look for a moment at a "negative case study."

In the year 2001, Enron implemented a strategy strongly promoted by McKinsey & Company, America's largest and perhaps most prestigious management consulting firm. McKinsey's research suggested that the most successful organizations waged what they called a "war for talent" in order to achieve high performance results. This war for talent strategy encouraged Jeffrey Skilling, the CEO of Enron, a former McKinsey partner himself, to encourage and set up hiring practices designed to attract and keep the very best talented candidates from all the best business schools. Skilling and Enron management believed in ranking people once per year into three groups — (As, Bs and Cs). The A's were challenged and rewarded disproportionately. The B's, although encouraged and rewarded did not receive anything like the rewards (bonuses/perks) of the A's. The C's were moved out. This approach at Enron – which I call "performance appraisal on steroids" created an unsupportable and ungovernable corporate culture, and contributed to the eventual, and inevitable chaos and disaster for which Enron is now best known. This "ABC" system allowed "super-star" heroes and heroines to run things the way they wanted — thereby creating competition, back-biting, and hoarding of information so they could achieve seemingly impossible goals "no matter what." This lack of coordination and cooperation is more common than most managers would care to admit, and although Enron is an extreme case, elements of this strategy can be seen in many firms today. Enron's strategy was not aligned with natural law. It was doomed to failure.

Although "talent," however you define it, is important, we do not need the most "talented" people in the marketplace for our organizations to be successful. We need people who are truly committed. This statement may appear to be a paradox to many.

"The words of truth are always paradoxical."

Lao Tzu

THE PARADOXES:

Leaders have a difficult job. They must live in a paradoxical world. (A paradox is a statement or statements that seem contradictory or absurd but reveal a possible new truth or insight.)

Here are a few paradoxes that leaders must learn to embrace:

- We want individual performance but not at the expense of organizational performance (i.e., beware of heroes or heroines).

- We want freedom, but we want to avoid chaos.

- We want strong leadership but we want to avoid tyranny.

- We want control but we don't want bureaucracies.

- We need to treat people differently but we don't have time to customize rules for everyone. We need one set of rules.

- We need to treat people fairly and equally but we also need to treat people differently since each person is unique.

- We must create performance and profit while achieving safety and quality.

- We want to have diversity but we must have the same rules and values for everyone.

A 2008 study of high performing organizations and their CEO's confirmed that effective leaders are able to reconcile and embrace the paradoxes that exist in their organizations.[1] When forming a strategic plan, CEOs who are most willing to be aware of the current reality and to hear the truth from their people will identify and resolve these paradoxes. This means being willing to hear the whole truth without shooting the messengers, engaging employees in the formulation of solutions by living clear values, engaging in long term thinking, creating a compelling aim for work, and creating an environment of trust. In such a workplace, the solutions to the paradoxes emerge through everyday work, and from constructive interactions between employees and management.

There is a balance within each paradox. Effective leadership seeks that balance. Just as a high wire act must make small and continuous adjustments to achieve a balance, the principles you will find in this book allow you to make those adjustments automatically and simultaneously.

Effective leaders need a management model to take the risks necessary to embrace these paradoxes. With the courage and insight that emerges through the lens of the most useful management theory and strategies, leaders will increase their probability of employee engagement and organizational success.

Embracing key principles – principles aligned with natural law — is the first critical step of a successful leader. You will learn those principles in this book.

Summary:

The system determines how good the player is.

A new way of thinking is needed if we are to achieve significant results.

CEOs must begin to recognize the paradoxes inherent in their line of work and embrace them.

CEOs need to be ready to change their own thinking first before they can expect to see significant results in the key areas of human motivation and productivity.

Now, more than ever, both hearts and minds of employees must be engaged because most workers today are knowledge workers. The accumulation of knowledge within each organization will improve profitability. The key is to engage every heart and mind, and thus increase the organizational knowledge level of the enterprise. We can do this. If we change our thinking it becomes simpler.

I believe that the key asset of successful firms lies inside the minds of their employees, and that the fundamental job of the leader lies in following Bill Walsh's example by creating a *system* that will enable each team member to reach his or her full potential. If you are interested in learning how to create such a system, for yourself and for your team ... read on.

(Endnotes)

1   Fredberg, T., Beer, M., Eisenstat, R., Foote, N., Norgren, F., 2008, *Forthcoming* Embracing Commitment and Performance: CEO's and Practices Used to Manage Paradox

Principle
ONE

A Leader's Responsibility: Manage the Context

Now it's time to take a look at the first of the three critical leadership principles I'll be sharing with you in this book. We can learn and embrace these principles, and when we do, we can truly make a difference as managers.

Principle #1: It's the leader's job to create the most useful context or environment.

Let me share a true story that will help to introduce this critical idea. Early in my consulting career, I helped facilitate an experiential team building retreat for a Pitney Bowes leadership team. The retreat was a two-day event; it featured a number of physical activities (such as rope climbing) that attempted to simulate important workplace issues. The purpose of the experiential activities was to create a context, observe team behavior, and relate an assessment of that behavior back to the workplace so the good behavior could be repeated and the poor behavior discarded. In theory, the new insights on individual and team behavior could be carried back to the workplace, and the resulting teamwork and improved relationships would become habit.

The event was fun and insightful, and certainly seemed to make a measurable difference in the relationships on the team. The petty conflicts and poor communications that pervaded the team prior to the retreat were mitigated (or at least seemed less critical).

The challenge with most of these types of trainings, though, is the lack of long-term sustainability of results and behavior change. Without a lasting change in the work context, the poor behavior often returns – because the context always influences the behavior.

Changing the context, I realized, is the key. A retreat, like the one we experienced, rarely if ever changes the context within which the team works. The retreat creates its own unique context, which creates new behaviors; those new behaviors are supposed to be transferred immediately to the workplace. The facilitators of the retreat, however, control the only the retreat context. The leaders of the organization control the workplace context.

To ensure long-term improvements in team and individual behavior, leaders must recognize their personal responsibility for changing the environment, or context, within which the behavior occurs.

CONTEXT IS EVERYTHING!

In January of 2007, during the morning rush hour , a 39-year-old violinist began playing at a subway station in Washington, D.C.

Not a particularly notable event, you might say. Actually, the morning performance was notable, because the musician was Joshua Bell, a renowned violinist and one of the top musicians in the world. The Washington Post and Mr. Bell had teamed up to conduct a social behavior experiment. Would people notice his exceptional music? Would they gather, wait and listen attentively, interrupting their busy commutes to hear a world-class musician play? Would they donate money? Or would they ignore him?

Bell played one of the most challenging and intricate classical pieces in his repertoire for 45 minutes. The instrument he played was a handcrafted Stradivarius violin valued at $3.5 million. Two days earlier, he had sold out a theater in Boston with seats costing an average of $100 each.

Yet over the course of the 45 minutes of exquisite music, only a handful of people actually slowed down to listen even briefly to him. Fewer still contributed. And fewer still stopped completely to spend a few consecutive moments taking in the extraordinary music. (Most of the people in this last category were children.) Bell collected a grand total of thirty-two dollars!

What does this experiment prove? One conclusion is: we cannot separate the individual's performance from the context. Did the dingy, damp, dark subway environment, with poor acoustics and poor lighting impact the perception of the quality of the of Bell's work? If the answer is yes (as the paltry amount of money Bell collected suggests), then isn't it true that the work environment can influence how people experience the quality of the work of the individuals within that workplace?

Leaders create and influence the work environment and, this change in context will inevitably change the meaning of events. This suggests that, as managers, we can't separate the performance of the individuals from the quality of the context within which they work.

The 2003 disintegration of the Columbia Space Shuttle was investigated by the independent Columbia Accident Investigation Board, which issued its findings in August 2003. The physical cause of the disaster was determined to be a flaw in the thermal protection tiles of the left wing. However, there is never just one cause for a problem in a complex system. The organizational causes of this disaster were rooted in NASA's history and a culture that allowed compromises, bowed to bureaucratic decision making, and prevented open and honest debate without fear of criticism.

This episode offers a major question for leaders: Are we focusing on the flaw in the thermal protection tiles ... or on the underlying cultural problems that made the flaw in the tiles possible?

We cannot separate behavior from the context. If we see behavior we don't appreciate, we must accept that any efforts to get employees to change behavior first will only create additional waste — in the form of lower morale, reduced productivity, reduced quality, and other problems — unless we are willing to change the context (that is, the environment) of the organization!

Very often, management blames only those few employees closest to the place where undesirable behavior first emerges. This is a classic (and usually serious) misjudgment. To understand why, consider the following true story.

A friend of mine was on a business trip and needed a few pieces of laundry cleaned. He placed the few critical pieces of clothing that he needed for a business meeting the following day into the hotel laundry bag and left it in the appropriate place for pick-up, expecting one-day service.

When the garments did not arrive the next morning, he called the front desk to inquire. He was told that his garments could not be located, but was assured they would be found and delivered as soon as possible. Hours went by, and he became angry with the service. He called to complain loudly, first to the service manager and then to the hotel general manager. After a thorough search, the laundry manager found the bag of cleaned laundry in an unmarked bag. Apparently my friend had forgotten to write his name and room number on the bag!

Understand: The laundry had gotten lost because of *my friend's* mistake. No amount of anger would change the fact that he himself had inadvertently created a dysfunctional context – and no doubt made it harder to solve the problem — by forgetting to fulfill his own responsibility. Many leaders inadvertently create a similar context of dysfunction, and then blame employees for the mistakes that occur.

Managers and leaders are inevitably the ones who have the most influence on the context of an organization. The context is whatever core assumptions are carried around in the minds of senior leadership; context always emerges from the belief system, or paradigm, of the owner.

Context is a matter of determining what questions get asked, and how loudly. If the question we are shouting is "Why did you idiots lose my laundry?" it may take us a while to penetrate to the specifics of the problem that actually exists on the ground.

Here is an example to demonstrate the importance of one's paradigm. In the space below, draw the Roman numeral "IX" (9) on a piece of paper. Now, drawing one line, turn it into a "6."

Answer on page 50.

Perhaps you were influenced to think about Roman numerals. As long as we think about Roman numerals we cannot solve the puzzle. Only when we stop thinking about artificially imposed limitations can we find a truly NEW solution. So it is with all of life's puzzles. Our assumptions limit our possibilities to find answers to the most challenging problems.

The context (environment) of an organization is created primarily by one thing:

The assumptions and beliefs of management.

In other words, management has a certain way of thinking about people and problems. The organizational environment is always profoundly affected by this habit of thinking.

This fundamental business truth is best illustrated by the Iceberg Model, which is based on the work of Donella Meadows. This model demonstrates how certain problems and issues overwhelm our focus, time and efforts as managers – and it also demonstrates the origin of those problems and issues.

The Iceberg Model

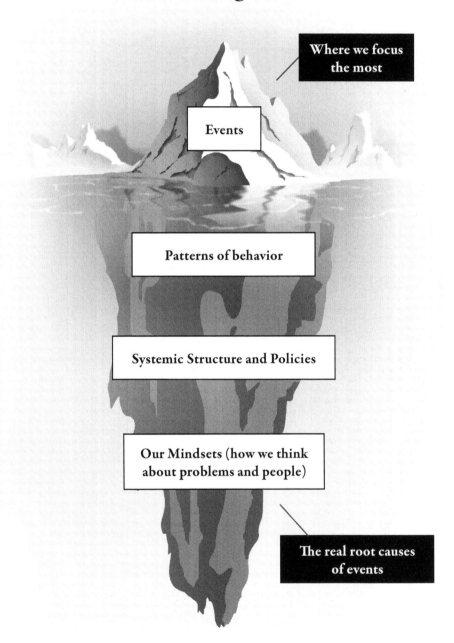

Where we focus
the most

Events

Patterns of behavior

Systemic Structure and Policies

Our Mindsets (how we think
about problems and people)

The real root causes
of events

An iceberg has 90% of its mass hidden below the surface. So it is with the root cause of issues we see manifest in the workplace. Managers often just try to fix the symptom that is clearly visible. But unless they address the root causes, the next symptom always rises to the surface. Suppose you could remove the top part of the iceberg – the part that's above the water surface. The act of removing it would of course require tremendous effort, but once you did that, the next ten percent would slowly rise above the surface!

The iceberg model demonstrates how problems or issues can overwhelm our focus, time and efforts at work. We all tend to put out fires that are caused by specific behaviors. The behaviors come from the policies, procedures, structure put in place by management. Those policies, procedures and structures are in turn formulated from management beliefs about people. For example: the less managers trust employees, the more policies and structure (bureaucracy) the organization requires to control behavior.

When my daughter Emily was in eighth grade, I was a chaperone for a school trip to Washington D.C. During the middle of the trip one of the students sent an inappropriate text message from his cell phone to a female student's cell phone. The teacher in charge of the trip was very upset. He demanded that everyone, even all parents, stop using their cell phones. He tried to "control" everyone's behavior with his command. This teacher created an immediate context of mistrust. His mistrust caused him to issue his "no cell phone use" policy. That policy caused, not the absence of cell phone use, but the *stealth* use of cell phones (especially by parents). The context of mistrust actually caused poor behaviors.

"All too often, management acts like a flea on an elephant. The flea barks out commands and sometimes the flea guesses correctly when it shouts, left, right, or stop. Sometimes, though, the barking flea doesn't guess correctly. The flea is either happy or upset based on the outcomes. The elephant, however, is indifferent and unaware."— *Anonymous*

If we want to evaluate the behavior of an individual, doesn't it make sense to do so considering the context in which the behavior occurs? For example, let's say an employee throws a temper tantrum during the workday. As it happens, this is the fifth time this month that Jacqueline has screamed at Bill, a co-worker. Is it most useful to report that employee to Human Resources for disciplinary action — or is it most useful to understand the context within which Jacqueline works to determine what can be done to avoid that behavior in the future? If we do this, we may find that there are deeper causes for the problem than we may have first recognized. For instance: Suppose Jacqueline's co-worker Bill has been withholding critical information that she needs to complete a project, despite repeated (private and respectful) reminders from her? Suppose that Bill perceives that management's attitude toward this behavior on Bill's part is basically tolerant – "Don't ask, don't tell"?

In this situation, do we really want to reprimand Jacqueline for screaming – which is indeed unacceptable — and send her off to HR? To do so may be to invite a complaint, or even a lawsuit! The real problem may be something else that is harder to perceive, but much more unacceptable: workplace harassment or incompetence.

THE ROOT CAUSE OF PROBLEMS IS MOST OFTEN IN THE CONTEXT

Leaders must decide to take personal responsibility for the context they create. The interaction of the vision, mission, values, strategy, and management paradigm all combine to create the full context that people experience on the job. It follows, then, that any leader who wishes to make significant changes in the way an organization operates must be willing to fix the foundation first ... not the roof.

Leaders must also begin to take personal responsibility for the environment they create. Every day, leaders create a working environment with the way they think, the way they express emotions, the way they make decisions, the way they communicate (behave) with their employees, and the way they communicate about strategic initiatives.

Context and environment are so closely interrelated as to be indistinguishable. And leaders are responsible for both halves of the equation.

SYSTEMS THINKING

Principle #1 brings us to an important personal and organizational insight: **Systems thinking can help create new opportunities to solve organizational problems.**

Let me explain. A system is a complex collection of interdependent processes that cooperate to achieve a specific aim or purpose.

There are at least three types of systems:

- Mechanical system: This system has parts that are interchangeable and act without choice. The control is from the outside and is accomplished by domination (on the part of the owner). A clock is an example of a mechanical system.

- Organism system: in this system, the parts exist only to provide the brain with inputs. All decisions and directions are made by the brain, and so the parts act without choice. Management of the organism is by command and control. The human body is an example of such a system.

- Social system: Here, there is an internal closed loop feedback process. The system is self-organizing and self-regulating. For the whole to be optimized the parts must cooperate, and they all have a choice. The management of the system is by influence only and not by control.

One metaphor that captures the essence of this model of change for modern organizations is "flocking birds."

Let's look a little more closely at the "flocking birds" model. It's mystifying to watch these dozens or even hundreds of birds, because they tend to move as one unit and somehow move in the same direction at more or less the same time. How and why do birds flock? There are three reasons — to find shelter, avoid predators, and to find food.

If they are working together cooperatively, and they're moving as one unit, then they can accomplish the three critical goals of that combined vision. How exactly do they do that?

As it turns out, birds have three basic principles hard-wired into their brains.

1) They fly in the same general direction as their closest neighbors.

2) They fly at the same average speed as their closest neighbors.

3) They fly at the same average distance from their closest neighbor, and thus avoid collisions.

By just following those three basic principles, they achieve their vision and they can make instant decisions as one unit — even though there is not one leader barking out demands to turn left or to turn right, to slow down or to speed up.

An effective organization, I believe, must operate in a very similar manner. An effective leader can create the proper context by recognizing the key foundational elements and working on those first.

According to a recent survey of 4,700 executives in 83 countries, the top two "people issues" that emerged in the workplace were:

- Managing talent

- Improving leadership

Many executives see talented people as one of the keys to organizational success. As we have discussed, talented people alone will not deliver the results executives seek (people are only as good as the system they play in) yet their belief in the need for talent continues to emerge as a desired success factor.

A useful metaphor for building a high performance organizational context is to imagine building a house.

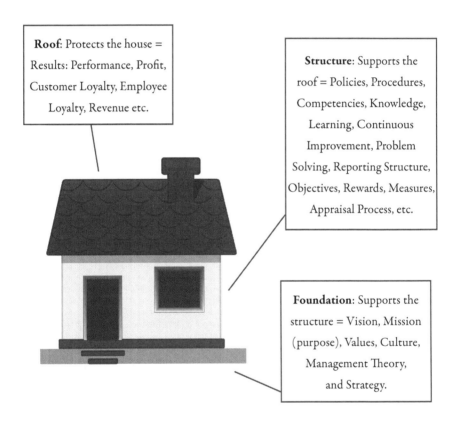

Roof: Protects the house = Results: Performance, Profit, Customer Loyalty, Employee Loyalty, Revenue etc.

Structure: Supports the roof = Policies, Procedures, Competencies, Knowledge, Learning, Continuous Improvement, Problem Solving, Reporting Structure, Objectives, Rewards, Measures, Appraisal Process, etc.

Foundation: Supports the structure = Vision, Mission (purpose), Values, Culture, Management Theory, and Strategy.

The Foundation = Vision, Mission, Values etc.

One of the first critical steps in house-building is to create a solid foundation. In a high-performance organization, the foundation includes the Vision (an ideal picture of a future state), the Mission (the purpose or aim; why the organization exists), the Values (the organization's intrinsically important priorities), Management Theory (how the senior leadership thinks about problems and people), and Strategy (the long-term plan of action). If each of these is clear and communicated to all employees, people tend to make decisions quickly and implement the structure.

The Structure = Policy and Procedure

The structure of an organization (analogous to the framing and walls of the house) is made up of all those things that put the items in the foundation into action. The structure is supported by the foundation. The more solid the foundation, the more stable the structure. The structure includes the Polices and Procedures (processes), Competencies (skills), Knowledge, Learning, Continuous Improvement, Problem Solving, Objectives, Rewards, and Measures. The performance appraisal process is one of the Polices and Procedures.

The Roof = Results

Finally, the roof is the results. The stronger the roof, the more the building is protected from the threatening elements of the environment. For an organization, these threatening elements include competitors, economy, government regulations, changing market conditions, changing customer expectations and demands, etc.

Leaders all want to see positive results. Precious resources will be wasted by trying to fix the roof when the real root cause of the problem is a weakened structure caused by a flawed foundation. This is why organizations frequently revise their performance appraisal process. On average, they do this every two years! The results are poor and so they "repair the structure" in an effort to "repair the roof" – over and over again. A better strategy is to reinforce the foundation, and then repair the structure.

A lack of alignment on the elements of the foundation can create tremendous barriers to growth and quality for an organization. Just as a house with a faulty or shaky foundation would be of poor quality and have major flaws in its structure, an organization with a lack of alignment in the elements of the foundation will be prevented from achieving optimal growth.

A solid foundation must be more than just the *creation* of the organizational Vision, Values, Management Theory, Culture, and Strategy for the organization. A successful leader must also know how to align people behind these things — by capturing both hearts and minds.

Hearts and minds are necessary prerequisites of commitment. True alignment of hearts and minds means people are happily willing to take action, be creative, solve problems, be pro-active and have all the other characteristics and behaviors that CEO's are looking for from their people.

Notice that the foundation must have all of the "bricks" in place (Vision, Mission or Purpose, Values, Culture, and Management Theory). These are all interdependent. Any weakness in one of these elements will create a weakness in the entire foundation. The Vision tells us where we are going. The Mission (or purpose/aim) tells us why we want to get there. The values and culture tell us how we are to behave and how we make decisions along the way. The management theory helps us to think and solve problems and remove barriers we encounter. Together, these things help us answer the basic questions: Where, How, Why, When, with Who?

A leader can create the proper context by working on the foundational elements first. Go back to the analogy of the flocking birds: A clear set of principles (foundation) will enable the organization to more quickly adapt to change and to perform optimally. With birds the foundation is the three key principles. With an organization it is the foundational elements of vision, mission, values, management theory, and strategy.

BIG CHANGES IN FREMONT

General Motors closed its Fremont, California plant in 1982. Why? Because out of all of its plants, the Fremont facility had the worst record for employee absenteeism, productivity, quality and morale. Then in 1983, in a joint initiative, Toyota and GM agreed to re-open the plant under two conditions: first, that the plant would be managed by Japanese-trained leaders; and second, 85% of all United Auto Workers who had worked at Fremont would be re-hired.

By 1991, that same plant, now renamed NUMMI (for New United Motors Manufacturing Inc.) had catapulted from having the worst track record to having the best in all the areas in which it had previously failed. What made the difference? The change was not attributable to "hiring problems," because the very same people who were once part of the failure had now became part of the NUMMI success story. The explanation for the turnaround lies in new a leadership style that used internal influence to change the methods people used to do their work. That new influence was rooted in a more collaborative style; it did away with the old "command-and-control" approach. The new leadership understood systems thinking.

The new thinking changed the methods which changed the environment, and that new environment produced positive results. The people were the same people. Only their thinking changed – and that is all that was needed to improve the results. Although NUMMI has since closed its doors (as of 2009), the closing was an outcome of the General Motors bankruptcy filing and not because of the plant's performance, which remained strong.[1] GM, a 50% owner of NUMMI, abruptly walked away from its contract. The abandonment of NUMMI by GM severely undermined the economic viability of the plant.

Because most school systems are based on a command and control mental model, and because most of us went to school, our tendency is to continue to embrace that philosophy when we begin working within and/or leading our organizations. Our belief system, as we have seen, has a strong effect on the choices we make in managing and leading people. This brings me to an important question:

What are your beliefs?

Obviously, this is a big question. If you answer the (slightly smaller) questions that follow, they will help you to find out what your beliefs are. Circle "Yes" or "No" after each one.

- **Question #1**: Will an improvement in individual performance by each employee lead to an improvement in overall organization improvement? (Yes/No)

- **Question #2:** Will evaluating individual employee performance during a performance evaluation improve the relationship with the employee? (Yes/No)

- **Question #3:** Is having a strong trusting relationship with an employee one of the most important factors in improving organizational performance? (Yes/No)

- **Question #4:** Will holding individual employees accountable for reaching their goals improve organizational performance? (Yes/No)

- **Question #5:** Can managers fairly and effectively evaluate employees without stereotyping and bias? (Yes/No)

- **Question #6:** Does holding employees accountable for individual goals help improve the performance of the entire organization? (Yes/No)

- **Question #7:** Will consistently and effectively conducting performance appraisals predictably improve employee motivation? (Yes/No)

Please do not turn the page until you have actually circled "Yes" or "No" in response to each of the questions you just read.

The answers to the questions you just read will begin to reveal your beliefs. Let me provide my answers to each question now, and then we can compare notes. We can then discuss why I believe what I believe ... and you can decide whether or not I am crazy.

That's not an uncommon reaction, by the way. Those individuals who do not agree with our beliefs can easily be seen as a crazy people. What's more, those individuals who do not agree with our values can appear crazy as well. In 1915 Albert Einstein formulated his Theory of Relativity. Based on that theory Einstein concluded that light could be bent by gravity. The scientists at the time were all proponents of Newtonian theory, which concluded this was impossible. Consequently Einstein was ridiculed in the scientific community. Many thought him quite insane.

In 1919, a team of researchers led by Sir Arthur Eddington conducted an experiment to measure the location of stars surrounding the sun during an eclipse. The precise measurements would either confirm or deny Einstein's predictions. Scientists everywhere were shocked when Eddington's results confirmed Einstein's predictions. The light from stars would "bend" as it passed by the sun, thus the position of the stars shifted ever so slightly. Einstein went from being a crazy person to a genius overnight.

The moral: Two people having different theories or beliefs can indeed appear quite crazy to each other.

Managerial practices can also appear to be a bit "crazy" if they are based on beliefs very different than our own. Please bear this in mind as you consider my responses to the questions you just answered; some may seem a bit crazy to you at first because of a possible significant gap in beliefs.

Question #1: "Will an improvement in individual performance by each employee lead to an improvement in overall organization improvement?"

A "yes" answer suggests the belief that a "whole" can be improved by improving the individual parts. A "no" answer acknowledges that the improvement of the parts is not enough to create improvement of the whole. In other words, something else is an influence on improvement. My answer is "no."

Most people who have been on a team that really "clicks," and compared this experience with being on a team that really doesn't, will agree with my answer.

The 1980 Olympics was forever marked in my memory when the USA Hockey Team won the Gold Medal in the final game against the Russians. That team was made up of a group of very talented individuals but those chosen were not necessarily the very best individual performers. The coach, Herb Brooks, chose players based on the potential for dynamic interaction between the players. He wanted each player to care more about the success of the team than about his personal success. "You're looking for players whose name on the front of the sweater is more important than the one on the back," Brooks once said. "I look for these players to play hard, to play smart and to represent their country."

The dynamic interaction between the parts is much more important than the quality of the parts. This is the fundamental belief that will cause someone to choose my answer, "no." A significant improvement in the parts can actually cause harm to the entire team. I would use the baseball scandal as the example. Those individual players who used steroids to improve their individual performance eventually hurt the entire team, Major League Baseball as a whole, and indeed the image of the entire national pastime.

Question #2: "Will evaluating individual employee performance during a performance evaluation improve the relationship with the employee?"

A "yes" answer suggests that someone who is judged by means of a performance evaluation will feel trusted and appreciated. A "yes" answer also suggests a belief that a performance evaluation can improve relationships. A "no" answer rejects both possibilities. I answer "no."

Research shows that performance evaluations do nothing to improve relationships and in fact probably damages trust between an employee and supervisor. Adecco Staffing of North America conducted a research study on this issue in March 2006. The results that showed of 2,000 people surveyed just 49% of the workers said they found that managers took performance appraisals seriously; only 44% said they received constructive feedback during performance appraisal. How can this type of result improve working relationships? A "no" answer acknowledges that criticism can indeed damage a relationship.

Question #3: "Is having a strong trusting relationship with an employee one of the most important factors in improving organizational performance?"

A "yes" answer suggests that relationships are critical to organizational performance. A "no" answer suggests that something else is more important. My answer here is "yes," an answer that rebuts the school of management exemplified by the sadly popular saying, "If you want a friend, get a dog."

Research from many sources shows that the higher the level of trust in an organization, the higher the level of performance in that organization is likely to be. If trust is a critical element to high performing organizations then developing strong trusting relationships must be a key factor.

Question #4: "Will holding individual employees accountable for reaching their goals improve organizational performance?"

A "yes" answer here suggests a belief that achieving individual goals is a key factor in organizational performance. A "no" answer rejects the idea that holding people personally accountable for attaining their goals will improve organizational performance. My answer is "no."

Holding people accountable means what? Many employees would answer that it means you get blamed when things don't go the way they should. What does accountable mean? Is it accepting responsibility? Should you accept responsibility for results when you don't have enough resources or authority to deliver the desired outcome?

As a young salesman I was assigned one of the largest accounts in our company: Gillette. This was a Fortune 500 company with high visibility and great influence on our business. I was lucky to be in the right place at the right time with this account; the people at Gillette had been working on a new product for two years; one month after my assignment to the account I was awarded a very large contract. Instantly I was seen as a sales genius because I had exceeded my goals.

I was asked to handle the large order; I had not been trained properly, however, and two months after winning the business, I came to find out that we were going to miss three important ship dates. There was nothing we could do but agree to custom-make new packaging on the dates Gillette was suggesting – an incredibly expensive and time-consuming option.

During the meeting where this issue was discussed, my boss kept glaring at me and giving me dirty looks. From his point of view, I had dropped the ball; I had ignored a problem and let matters drift to a point where the company would have to incur a great deal of overtime to accommodate the orders.

I was a hero one week, and then two months later I was a bum. Why? because there were factors outside of my control. I had made an important sales goal but I had failed to schedule the order properly because of a lack of training. No one had ever shown me how to schedule the order.

Yes, I was naive and inexperienced, but that's not the most important lesson of the story.

The fact that anyone could go from being a hero to a bum in just two months tells me I should not have been held accountable for this mistake. Why should I have been "held accountable" for something I didn't understand and had never been taught how to do? For that matter, why should I have received accolades for an order that fell into my lap?

Why should I have been blamed for a mistake (namely, poor planning) when I was completely unaware of what I should do? Sure, I could have asked better questions. Perhaps I should have thought about the situation more deeply. Would lecturing me about those points really help the organization avoid this type of situation in the future? Would "holding me accountable" for my mistake really help the organization in the future? Would the fear of punishment help future young sales people more than improvements in the training process would?

Leaders often don't want to hear this, but most root causes of employee errors can be traced back to the context, and specifically to a policy, process, or decision controlled by leaders.

Question #5: Can managers fairly and effectively evaluate employees without stereotyping and bias?

A "yes" answer here suggests that managers can be objective in their evaluation of individual employees. A "no" answer suggests that managers can't help but have a positive bias toward those employees they like and a negative bias toward those they dislike. Which do you think is true? What has been your experience?

My answer is "no," because I believe that mangers are inevitably biased toward employees they like, and against employees they do not like.

If your son or daughter worked for you, wouldn't you have to address the possibility of personal bias toward them over another non-family member who reported to you? Perhaps that's an extreme example. Perhaps it's also an instructive one. Mahzarin Banaji, author of "How (Un)ethical Are You?," argues that unconscious bias is unavoidable.

Mr. Banaji's claim is that our brains naturally cause our bias and do so at an unconscious level. Because we function most often on an unconscious level in everyday activities, our natural tendency is to behave according to our bias. Even the most well meaning person in the world will succumb to this weakness, because the human brain works on the basis of associations.

Banaji writes: "Good managers often make unethical decisions and don't even know it .... most fair-minded people strive to judge others according to their merits, but our research shows how often people instead judge according to unconscious stereotypes and attitudes, or implicit prejudice."

If we can't trust ourselves to be unbiased, how can we possibly judge another's job performance? The shortest and best answer is that we can't. Instead we must help people collect data that allows them quick feedback without needing a manager's approval or evaluation. This provides a greater opportunity for quick decision making and provides a system-dependent way for people to manage their own work.

THE SPOUSE TEST

If you still believe that managers can fairly evaluate their own employees, I suggest that you try this simple exercise. When you go home tonight and talk to your spouse or significant other, tell him or her you are ready to deliver an annual Performance Appraisal. Tell him or her you have some great suggestions for improving overall performance and household operation. What kind of reception will you get? Will you be able to remove any pre-existing bias with this approach? Will performance improve? Will the relationship improve?

Question #6: "Does holding employees accountable for individual goals help improve the performance of the entire organization?"

A "yes" answer suggests managers and employees are smart enough to choose specific goals that will improve the organization. It also suggests that the employees are skilled enough to achieve the goals set by management. In other words, manager and employees would have to see a way to satisfy customers, employees, investors and other stakeholders by choosing exactly the right goals and providing awards to employees for achieving the goals and consequences for not achieving them. A "no" answer suggests there are other factors that will help the organization be successful. I say "no."

My "no" answer acknowledges the difficulty of knowing all the right answers in a complex system.

Employees concerned about receiving a bad rating or being held accountable for a goal (especially one tied to compensation) will likely put their own welfare ahead of others, even at the expense of the customer's welfare.

Question #7: "Will consistently and effectively conducting performance appraisals predictably improve employee motivation?"

A "yes" answer suggests performance appraisals are a valuable tool. It also suggests that people need to be motivated by managers evaluating them.

A "yes" answer conflicts with much significant data. The Watson & Wyatt WorkUSA® 2004 study, for instance, revealed that only three out of ten U.S. workers say their company's performance management program actually does what it intends to do — improve performance. And only two out of ten workers say their company helps poorly performing workers improve. In addition, the Society for Human Resource Management (SHRM) in one of their studies found that 90% of performance appraisal systems are unsuccessful! A 1997 survey by Aon Consulting and SHRM reported that only 5% of companies were very satisfied with their company's performance management systems.

I answer "no" to this question because I believe that employees are not motivated by being given a grade by their manager. I believe they are motivated by other factors that have nothing to do with performance appraisals and everything to do with other key factors. These factors include:

- Having control of their choices and being empowered to make those choices.

- Receiving meaningful and timely feedback.

- Doing interesting work that clearly makes a difference and is consistent and connected with a higher purpose other than just receiving a reward.

- Seeing how they are making a difference in the world.

It is doubtful that performance appraisals can provide these factors.

I feel it is likely that other processes than performance evaluations can deliver on these factors, and therefore my answer to Question #7 is "no."

Simply put, performance appraisals don't accomplish their purposes because they are inconsistent with systems thinking. Organizations are systems and systems are complex collections of interdependent processes intended to achieve the mission or aim of the organization. The existence of performance appraisals assumes the individual parts (people) can act independent of the system. They cannot.

The New Administrative Assistant

Consider the true story of a new administrative assistant who was hired and then quickly placed on probation for "unacceptable performance levels." She was asked to perform with minimal training; her co-workers were asked to observe her and evaluate her performance. Her performance suffered; she is eventually let go and replaced with another candidate who performed well enough to be hired and hold on to the job.

Was the first candidate a "poor performer" – or was she more negatively impacted by the prevailing system than the second candidate? Could her performance be evaluated separate from the context in which she had to work? Was the lack of proper training a factor? Possibly the workload was different for her than the second candidate. What about the hiring process? Was that a factor in this situation? What about the method of evaluation? Did the co-workers show any bias toward one candidate and less bias toward the other? How could we know for sure?

Performance appraisals give each employee an overall grade that often determines their pay and/or promotional opportunities. Improving individual parts of a system is an ineffective and potentially damaging approach to improving performance in a system because the real root causes of poor performance are never adequately addressed. Very often, the factors that caused the first candidate to leave are not addressed by the hiring of the second candidate!

(Endnotes)

1   http://www.toyota.com/about/news/manufacturing/2010/03/03-1-nummi.html

There are two answers to the example on page 26: *SIX or 1 X 6.*

Principle
TWO

A Leader's Way of Thinking:
The Values and System Model

Our second leadership principle draws on what we have learned from the first: The way leaders think determines environment, which in turn determines organizational behavior.

Let's begin our discussion of this vitally important leadership principle by explaining an essential question: *Why* does the way a leader thinks about people and problems determine the decisions they make and the policies they embrace? *Why* do management's prevailing theories determine management policies, procedures and behaviors?

When leaders embrace a certain management model, that model determines the unique *environment* of the organization. This environment will do one of two things. It will either provide greater encouragement and opportunity for employees ... or it will create an environment of distrust and inaction.

The continued and consistent behavior of leaders influences the way all the people in the organization *think* about the organization and its problems. Only a leadership "thinking change" will shift the culture from one of paralysis into one of increased trust. One barrier to this shift toward trust is the embrace of faulty beliefs.

Beliefs play a critical role in our ability to achieve results. Beliefs can do one of three things.

- Enhance our ability to achieve
- Be neutral
- Prevent us from achieving.

Beliefs have a major impact on the elusive workplace quantity known as "attitude." Let's consider the word "attitude" for a moment. A high percentage of professional speakers, probably a majority, make their living reminding their audiences that "It's not what happens to us that matters it is how we react to it that counts!" In other words, we can control our attitude.

People with poor attitudes can always be found in a poor performing organization. The question is: Do the people arrive first and create the poor organization ... or does the poor organization create the attitudes? A clear definition of the word "attitude" may help us to help make sense of the paradox.

I believe there are three elements to attitude:

1. How we think about a given issue (our belief).

2. How we feel about it (our emotion)

3. What we do – or choose not to do (our action)

Thus, attitude is really three things, not just one. This fact helps us to get a better understanding of "attitude problems" within our organization. We don't consciously *hire* people with poor attitude, do we? Of course not. Quite the contrary: We consistently hire people with great attitudes – or so it seemed at the time. Yet if – as is often the case — we hire people with good attitude and their attitude changes, we have to ask ourselves: what happened? One answer is that something in the environment influenced how they felt about something, how they felt about it, and/or what they did (or didn't do) in response.

The following true story illustrates how a poor environment – or context – can shift attitudes. Remember please, as you read it that it is the *leader's* job is to manage the context.

BELIEFS ON THE JOB

A while back, my daughter Emily was hired by a local outlet of a national clothing chain. She was so excited; this was her first "real job." She had been hired on the spot right after her first interview. She felt so pleased with herself, and went into her first day confident she would do a good job. Why? Because management was obviously appreciative of her attitude. The hiring officer had also praised her skills in dealing with people and her communication skills.

After two weeks on the job, Emily came home from work looking dejected and disgusted; I asked her how her shift had gone. She said, "Those managers are so stupid! They are only concerned about making money for themselves. I'm not getting the help I need. It's been two weeks, and no one has shown me how to process checks!" This was a big problem, because she was working on the cash register.

"I had two people write checks today and it took me forever to figure it out on the fly. People were waiting in line and began to be upset with me. I wish they had taken more time to help me learn how to do the checks."

Her attitude had been impacted by the lack of training. She was thinking the managers should have helped her learn how to do the job. She was feeling very embarrassed and frustrated that she had not gotten the training she deserved. She was looking very beaten-down and upset. She now had a bad attitude. How did I know that? Well, she was showing her attitude in her body language and her tone of voice; what's more, the words she chose which were not very complimentary to management.

Why couldn't she control her attitude? Why couldn't she just brush it off and smile and say, "Oh well, I will do better next time?" Because the environment influenced her attitude. Her belief about management and her expectations about management's role and responsibility created a feeling of frustration. That manifested in disgust, embarrassment and, last but not least, anger for having been embarrassed.

Beliefs create expectations. Expectations and observations and experiences inevitably impact attitude. We can control how we behave in certain situations but we can't really control our beliefs in the moment (although they can change over time). Our beliefs are usually set, and we create our expectations based on those beliefs.

BELIEFS AND OUTCOMES

There are two classic examples that show how belief can have a major effect on an outcome: the placebo effect and the Pygmalion effect. Let's look at each.

The placebo effect describes a common experience in the world of medicine. A doctor provides an inert chemical, such as a sugar pill, to a patient who then exhibits a therapeutic benefit. The outcome is as widespread as it is mysterious.

Despite decades of study and theorizing, no one really understands how a placebo works. What is known is that there are usually two important factors present when a positive health effect occurs: first, the authority figure (typically a doctor) administers the "treatment;" and second, the patient truly believes the treatment will work. The placebo provides no chemical reaction to explain the therapeutic effect. The only operating factor appears to be the belief created by the authority figure and/or the patient. Such is the power of a belief. The patient improves simply because he or she believes in the treatment and/or in the authority figure.

Although there is still great controversy about placebos, it seems misguided to deny the possible beneficial effect of a positive belief.

It seems equally misguided to deny that the inverse is also true in medicine. Even if given an effective drug, without the benefit of a strong belief, the possible beneficial effects will not be realized by the patient and he/she will probably not improve.

A story described by Abraham Maslow can demonstrate this. According to Maslow, a psychiatrist was treating a man who believed he was a corpse. The treatments had gone on for many weeks and the doctor had made zero progress to convince the patient he was in fact alive and not dead. The doctor was quite frustrated but was undaunted and thought of a great new approach. The doctor, in a final attempt to convince the patient otherwise asked a few questions: He asked, "Does a corpse bleed?" "Of course not", replied the patient. "Corpses can't bleed." After asking permission the doctor pricked the finger of the patient. When the blood began to flow, the patient was astonished. "Oh my," he said at last. "I guess I was wrong. Corpses do bleed."

As the placebo effect demonstrates, beliefs create expectations and therefore impact feelings and actions. Beliefs can be either a benefit or a road block. If you as a leader are frustrated with your people or your organization, it is important for you to explore how your beliefs may be affecting your stated or unstated expectations – and how those expectations may be affecting our feelings and your employees' behaviors.

The Pygmalion Effect is a great example of how beliefs can create expectations and specific results. This effect refers to the way the expectations of someone else can determine our performance.

The most well known version of the story is found in the play *Pygmalion* by George Bernard Shaw, subsequently adapted into the musical *My Fair Lady*. In the play the main character, Henry Higgins, makes a bet with his friend that he can pass off a poor, ill-spoken girl as a woman from high society simply by teaching her how to speak differently. The change in speech, he argues, will create an expectation by others in high society that she is "one of them" – and as a result she will be treated like a woman of means.

This Pygmalion Effect is not just a story. It is an observed phenomenon in studies that measure the effect of expectations of teachers on their students. One particularly compelling study showed how the expectations of elementary school teachers affected the results of the children they taught. Two elementary classes were switched. One teacher, who expected high performing students with high intelligence, was switched with another teacher, who expected a classroom full of trouble makers with low I.Q.'s. The teachers were not informed of the switch until after the end of the school year. Significant increases in performance were seen with the low IQ kids. Significant reduction in performance was seen with the high IQ kids. No other change was made – and therefore, one can conclude, the expectations of the teachers were the major factor in the shift in performance.

The Free Throw

Dr. Tom Amberry knows how to throw a free throw. On November 15, 1993, he set the world record for most consecutive free throws sunk, with 2,750 straight baskets from the foul line. It took him 12 hours; he had ten witnesses who signed affidavits, enabling Guinness to recognize his accomplishment in its famous Book of World Records. He could have kept going, but the gym was closing and the management asked him to leave!

Is Amberry incredibly talented, or does he have a process that anyone can use? Actually, he has a two-part process. First, he has strict mechanics. "It's important to have the right mechanics. Once you learn to put your body in the proper position and shoot correctly, then the rest is mental," says Dr. Tom.

Amberry has total focus and concentration, which is the second part of his process. He thinks of only making the free throw and blocks out all else from his mind. In addition, he thinks only positive thoughts about the basket and is 100% positive that he can make it.

This two-step process can be mastered by virtually anyone motivated to master it. After only one coaching session with Dr. Tom, an assistant coach sank 68 free throws in a row – and the very next day improved to 98 in a row. The Cal State Bakersfield Roadrunners went from a 62% to 83% free throw average in just one game. In only one week a group of players in junior high was able to achieve an 80% average after only one week of practice!

What are we to conclude from all this? For one thing, the process makes a major difference in individual performance. If that is true, and it seems undeniable that it is, *why not evaluate the process and help people to follow a good, predictable process ... instead of evaluating the individuals?*

After all, if we use the performance evaluation system to send people the message that we have "evaluated" them and found fault with them, aren't we sending the same underachieving message that the teachers who thought they were teaching below-average IQ students sent their kids? How much better off would everyone be if we evaluated the *process* our people were using, and tweaked it until it was as solid as Dr. Tom's?

The performance improvement can be significant when there is a strategy of a) developing a predictable process and b) helping others to follow that process. The Values and System Management model helps us to do this in an organization.

What have we learned thus far? A leader's main job is to manage the context of the organization. The context is determined mainly by the way the leader thinks. A leader's beliefs will determine how a leader thinks. Beliefs are limiting. In order to change performance of people and of organizations leaders must challenge their own thinking.

Systems thinking helps us to explain how a leader must think in order to optimize performance. Systems thinking demands that leaders focus their attention on improving the quality of interactions between people instead of improving the performance of individuals. Improving individual performance will not insure the improvement of organizational performance.

When fear is reduced and trust is increased, employees will naturally become more committed to their work, to their organization, and to delivering value to their customers.

All of this gives rise to a question. If fear is so damaging and trust is so helpful to organizations, why haven't people simply stopped the behaviors that cause fear?

Fear is persistent in organizations because employees and managers *both* assume the other is only focused on their own personal self-interest. Furthermore, they believe one's success is often purposely at the expense of the other's success (a zero-sum game). Any policy or procedure that reinforces this assumption will inevitably be a barrier to trust.

Trust is a critical element of every interaction in an organization. It creates the foundation for quality, performance, and profit. Like any foundation, if it is solid, it allows the organization to grow with confidence and consistency. **Any policy or process that may undermine this foundation of trust must be corrected permanently.**

As we have seen, the typical Performance Appraisal is just such a policy. If we are to change the existing performance appraisal pattern, and implement the ideas I am proposing in this book, I believe we must come to terms with this dysfunctional policy.

DUNKIN' DONUTS®: A TRUE STORY

I love Dunkin' Donuts Coffee. Nearly every morning I will pick up a large cup just before a client meeting and bring it into the meeting with me. I always order a large decaf and I don't like sugar. For years, I ordered my coffee using this process: "May I have a large decaf, cream, no sugar."

About 10 % of the time I would get sugar in my coffee. Since I can't drink coffee with sugar, I would have to either toss it out and be out $2.00 or go back and order another. The Dunkin' Donuts were always friendly about replacing the coffee, even if, as often happened I was cranky about the mistake; it was just a hassle to go back and replace it.

One day I ordered a coffee, got in my car and headed to my appointment. I tasted the coffee; sure enough, it had sugar. I got angry. I decided to go back and complain loudly about how they don't seem to hire people who can listen at Dunkin' Donuts. By the time I got to the store, however, the possible implications of confronting the store manager with an emotional outburst had begun to give me pause.

Perhaps my own process was not working. Why was I mentioning sugar at all if I didn't want any sugar?

I decided at that moment to change my process. I began asking for a "Large Decaf — just cream." In the four years since I changed my process, I have not gotten sugar in my coffee a single time. Not once!

As it turns out, human brains have a difficult time hearing a negative. If you ask someone to stop thinking about pink rabbits, they will think about pink rabbits. If you ask for no sugar, they will hear sugar.

It was the mention of sugar (the process) that caused the problem. The Dunkin' Donuts worker was not the root cause. My system was the root cause. Once I changed the process the problem disappeared.

Furthermore, once I asked a system question such as "What is the first 15% of the process?" I was able to solve the problem without upset.

The first 15% of receiving coffee the way I want it (just cream) is the ordering process which I control. Once I realized I contributed to the error (sugar) I could change my process and avoid the upset.

THE VALUES AND SYSTEMS MODEL

My Values and Systems Problem Solving Model is based on research by Rob LeBow, William Simon, and Dr. W. Edwards Deming. Simply stated, their research suggests that when faced with an organizational problem, leaders need to begin by asking one question: Is this problem a values issue, or systems issue?

Rob LeBow and William Simon's research correlate with that of Dr. Deming. In their book *Lasting Change*, they describe how values create the context of the organization and lay the foundation for lasting changes (transformation). They asked a simple question: "What do people want in their work environment in order to be more productive and to perform at the top of their game?" Here's how they went about answering that question.

"Our team spoke to and interviewed dozens of business people, HR professionals, instructional designers, business consultants, training companies, researchers, business leaders, CEO's, organizational development specialists ... After all the searching, we knew that no person or organization had a satisfactory answer. Finally we stumbled upon a research project that had begun at the University of Chicago, in which the team had collected 17 million surveys of workers in 40 countries around the world on what people wanted in their work environments to be productive, creative, fulfilled, and competitive" (Lebow & Simon, 1997).

The answer came back as "Shared Values."

The respondents of this survey mentioned truth, trust, openness, honesty, respect, risk taking, mentoring, giving credit and caring as those things they could all agree need to be in the environment. The result of an environment with these values is freedom and a lack of fear. This freedom allows employees to focus on problem solving. They begin to realize they have the power to influence change in themselves, their managers and their processes (the system).

LeBow and Simon also agree with Deming's premise that people can be trusted because they already want to do a good job. They are not, contrary to popular belief, lacking motivation; instead, they lack an environment and tools that would allow them to be motivated naturally. LeBow insists people should be trusted because the trust will allow them to be great, something they already want to be. They can do without management coercion or interference to create motivation.

The University of Chicago survey data specifically mentions values such as honesty, truth and trust. People already want these and they don't need to be forced or controlled to want them. The survey respondents are telling us their environments don't support the values they desire in order to do a good job. People want to be trusted. They want the ability to offer the truth and they want to be respected.

These values once shared must somehow come to life. Without the corresponding behavior that is congruent with these values, employees can't see or feel the transformation. The values must be lived everyday by employees and management. *"Shared values are in essence not what we say they are. The values of an organization are how people behave everyday. Behaviors in a shared values environment are judged by fellow employees, management, and the company's customers"(Lebow & Simon, 1997).*

Shared values positively impact profit. For example, LeBow studied business and financial results for eight restaurants. Some had implemented his shared values process and others did not. He ranked them in financial performance using net income before operating expenses, performance against plan and profitability. Those with the most positive work environment (who had implemented his shared values approach) were the ones at the top of the financial performance. There was a correlation with financial performance and positive work environment.

A values issue involves a purposeful break in integrity such as lying, sabotage, being disrespectful or failing to follow through on a commitment or agreement. Problems that are values issues are behavioral, which means individuals have choices as to how they can react or behave. For example, telling or not telling the truth is a choice. Being respectful in the face of disrespect is a choice. Values issues are very serious because they create an emotionally charged environment, which puts relationships at risk.

Simply stated, their research suggests that when faced with an organizational problem, leaders need to begin by asking one question: Is this problem a values issue, or systems issue?

In the Values and Systems problem-solving model, every problem that is not a values issue is a systems issue. Problems that result from systems issues include: mistakes, oversight, forgetting, poor training, poor quality, poor performance or lack of motivation.

More often than not, the root of a problem is due to a problem with a system, but it manifests itself on the surface as a "people" problem.

The Values and System Problem-Solving Model

When there is an issue, it is either a values issue or a system issue.

Values Issue	Systems Issue
Break in integrity	Mistakes
Intentional mistake	Errors or oversights
Disrespect	Poor quality - variation
Intentional break in policy	Poor attitude
Blaming others	Poor performance
Excuses	Lack of motivation
Not taking responsibility	Not understanding responsibility
	Inadequate Training
	Ineffective policies

In the Dunkin Donuts story I shared with you a little earlier, I was very tempted to be disrespectful to the manager and the server. In other words, I nearly broke values.. By following the Values and System Model, I realized that I was contributing to the mistakes that were bothering me, and that my reacting disrespectfully would be worthless. Instead, I needed to look at the first 15% of my process to find the real root cause.

THE HIGHWAY

The Values and System model I am proposing is completely consistent with systems thinking. To demonstrate this, all we need to do is think of a highway. A highway has a purpose or aim: to provide an area of safe travel for automobiles from one place to another. A highway is a system because it is a series of interdependent processes that are intended to achieve an aim. Each person driving to work in the morning can be considered one part of the overall highway system. Driving an automobile is a process; each person driving on the highway can be considered a process. The road conditions, the traffic lights, the signs, the quality of maintenance, the design of the exit ramps — all of these are parts of the system. Each part impacts the other parts because they are interdependent. **Attempting to evaluate only one part of a system ignores the interaction of one part to another.**

THE NEW CAR

Now imagine you're going to buy a new car. You research which car manufacturer makes "the very best" for each of the different parts. You buy only "the very best parts" from each of the manufacturers. Perhaps you choose a chassis by Chevy, an engine from Chrysler, an interior from Ford, and headlights from Honda. You choose the parts for one reason and one reason alone: because they are the BEST! You put all the parts in a warehouse. You hire a couple of engineers. You tell them to put the parts together — because the very best parts will create the very best vehicle. When the engineers put everything together, will the "new car" work?

I say no. Why? Because the quality of the interaction between the parts is far more important than the quality of the individual parts. As a general but very reliable rule, a performance appraisal attempts to improve the individual quality of the parts ... and completely ignores the quality of the interactions between the person and the system. In any system, improving the quality of the interactions is critical to achieving high performance.

The Values and System Model enables successful leaders to harness the constructive power of an effective system, move away from blaming people, and find innovative solutions to complex problems.

In this management model, unclear or dysfunctional processes are the real root cause of most, if not all, people problems or human conflict within organizations. Uncovering the system issue requires patience and tools. It requires thinking clearly. Too often management jumps to the conclusion that people are the cause. By embracing the Values and System Management Model, a successful leader will continue to explore ways to improve the system and will interpret emotional upsets as an opportunity to uncover serious system issues. Occasionally, we may conclude that individual people are seriously flawed and are the cause of a given problem. This is rare, however, and when it does occur it probably means the hiring process was flawed.

The following story illustrates how hidden root causes within the system must be identified.

The Laboratory

My client, the administrator of a water-testing laboratory, asked me to work with the manager of the laboratory, who was having serious problems with the eight chemists that he managed. The administrator wanted me to work with the manager on his communication skills. The administrator hoped that doing so would help to improve the manager's relationships with his staff.

In my first meeting with the manger, the manager told me that the lab performed testing on samples for a state environmental agency. As the manager of the laboratory, one of his responsibilities was to make sure there were no errors in the lab reports before they went back to the state. He said that he repeatedly found errors in the test reports, and that he was trying to get the chemists to be more careful.

I asked the manager what he did when he found that a mistake had been made. He told me that he immediately identified which chemist made the error. When he did, he approached the responsible person, pointed out the mistake, and then asked, very nicely, that the chemist be more careful in the future. This process had been going on for some time, and there had apparently been no improvement. The manager was frustrated and the chemists were irritated with the manager. The chemists felt that they were under stress, consistently having to work long hours, and they resented being "attacked" by the manager.

In an attempt to get to the root of the problem, I sat down with the manager and together we reviewed the errors. The manager said that he had scrutinized the data time and time again, looking for patterns and finding none. He had to assume that the problem was caused by human error; so with the best of intentions, he kept reminding the chemists to be more careful.

Together, we still found nothing, not even a clue about the source of the problem. At that point, I asked the manager, "What is the very first thing the chemists do when they prepare to test something?" I encouraged him to engage the chemists to get the answer. They told us the first thing they did was to go and get clean glassware from the glass-cleaning department.

We then went to the glass-cleaning department. There we found two old dishwashing machines in poor condition. We also discovered that the person in charge of the glass cleaning process was new to the position and had not been properly trained. Next, we analyzed the condition and cleanliness of the glassware that was waiting to be sent to the lab. After a thorough investigation, we were astonished to find an invisible film on the inside of some of the glassware. Once we discovered the film, we were able to make a direct connection between the appearance of the film and the errors in the data.

To correct the problem, we created a training process for the glass cleaning person. We created a maintenance schedule for the dishwashing equipment, and the film disappeared. So did the errors! After that, the relationships between the chemists and the manager began to improve.

The manager stopped sending the message that the chemists were at fault for the errors. The errors were a system issue and not a values issue.

The relationships between the manager and chemists improved along with the quality and productivity of the laboratory. By solving the system issue, the root cause of the "people problems" was uncovered and corrected.

> "If you do not know how to ask the right question, you discover nothing...What we need to do is learn to work in the system, by which I mean that everybody, every team, every platform, every division, every component is there not for individual competitive profit or recognition, but for contribution to the system as a whole on a win-win basis."
>
> Dr. W. Edwards Deming

The Values and System Management Model can be applied as well to problems and conflict that appear at home.

The School Bus

When my daughter Emily was 12, she had difficulty catching the school bus. Here is what I heard almost every morning from my wife. She said, "Emily, hurry up; you're going to miss the bus. What's going on? You're not dressed? You're going to miss the bus. You are so disorganized. You better get your act together. Where are your books?"

This went on for about five or six weeks; One morning, she came running downstairs to my office in tears and said, "Dad, you have to take me to school; I missed the bus again.' I tried to calm her down. I said, "Okay, honey, I am happy to take you to school, but I want you to take a deep breath and help me with this question. What's the system issue that caused you to miss the bus?" She said, "Dad, I don't know what you're talking about." I said, "What's your method of catching the bus?" Frustrated, Emily asked, "Can't you just take me to school?"

I said, "You don't have a process to catch the bus and so Mom is yelling at you, which is disrespectful. Because you don't have a process or method to catch the bus Mom is angry and frustrated and so are you."

I continued, "What I would like you to do is to figure out a way that you can catch the bus on your own and Mom will stop yelling.' She rolled her eyes and said, "Alright Dad, fine." I drove her to school.

I was pleasantly surprised when she came home that night because she said, "*Dad, I thought of something. If you buy me one of those egg timers, I will set it on the kitchen table and I will set it for five minutes ahead and when it goes off, I know I have 5 minutes to get ready to catch the bus.*"

I asked her to make an agreement with me to set the timer at breakfast each school morning as she had described. She agreed.

She did that for the last three of her grade school years. She never once missed the bus after that. The morning yelling sessions stopped as well.

By solving the system issue, the root cause of the "people problems" was addressed.

When managers embrace the Values and System Model, they change the environment of the organization. The changed environment provides greater encouragement and opportunity for managers and employees to change their behaviors. The continued and consistent behavior changes influences the way people think about organizational problems. The thinking change shifts the culture into a "culture of increased trust."

THE EARLY CHRISTMAS PRESENT

Recently, I was on a business trip a couple weeks before Christmas. I called home and my 17-year-old daughter answered the phone. She sounded happy and excited. She said: "Dad, guess what? Joe (her boyfriend) gave me by Christmas present early. Guess what it is." I remember my heart skipped a beat as I realized there were multiple items on the list of things that I feared it might be. One item on my "fear list" for example was a weekend in NYC alone with Joe.

I said, "I have no idea, honey. What is it?"

She said, "A puppy!"

My heart sank, even though I was relieved it was not the trip to New York City.

"That is quite a gift!" was all I could muster. I was thinking about how I might choke Joe. Would it be from behind or from the front? I couldn't decide.

My daughter went on to explain how surprised she was and how excited too. The puppy was so cute. He was an eight-week-old Beagle. Obviously I was upset with Joe because the gift of the dog was not just a gift to my daughter. It was a gift to the entire family. The gift impacted our entire system.

Clearly, Joe did not have our system in mind when he purchased the puppy. Who was going to purchase the food, take him out at 6 a.m. in the cold, walk him around the block, and clean up his messes? I had a feeling it was not just going to be my daughter.

Very often, decisions are made that impact the entire system and often the leaders of organizations do not see their impact unless they appreciate a system.

The Firestone/Ford Argument

In the year 2000, the auto tire giant Bridgestone/Firestone recalled 6.5 million Wilderness AT tires. Huge numbers of Ford Explorers had been equipped with these tires over the years; it emerged that the Explorers had been involved in a significant number of rollover accidents in which 170 people had lost their lives and over 700 had sustained significant injures. Firestone and Ford had been throwing barbs at each other for some time already about who was responsible for the problems. Eventually, the tires had to be taken off the market - and off the Explorers. The public was losing confidence in both companies.

What happened here? Which company was at fault? If you go back and read the news stories, you>ll find that it was never entirely clear which firm was to blame. They both made compelling arguments. A definitive answer was never found.

This is often the case in a complex system, where solutions must come from cooperation and quality interactions. The two companies were so concerned about avoiding liability that they forgot to focus on improving the quality of the interdependent interactions.

The Values and Systems model enables successful leaders to begin to fully appreciate the real-world possibilities within such a system, move away from blaming people, and find innovative solutions to complex problems. As explained earlier, a leader's beliefs about people and problems will inevitably determine the policies and practices, which will in turn, determine the results of an organization.

In other words: It all starts with thinking.

(Endnotes)

1   Paradox: two seemingly opposite ideas seeming to be true at the same time

Principle
THREE

A Leader's Strategy: Managing Trust

Principle #3: A leader must consciously and continuously manage trust with all constituents.

To implement this principle, we have to understand what workplace trust is. My aim here is twofold: to define trust in the workplace accurately, and to make the case for a strategic initiative to continuously improve workplace trust in each and every organization. To do both of those things, I need to share another personal story about trust.

One day, my wife Lori asked me to install a new kitchen faucet. I am pretty handy around the house, so I agreed. I asked her to come with me to the Home Depot to choose the right faucet to install.

At Home Depot, we found an entire wall of faucets and looked through them for at least 45 minutes before choosing one that we liked. I was so grateful that Lori had come with me, because I knew there was no way I would have had the competence to choose the "correct" one on my own.

I had the faucet; now I had to decide what was needed for the installation. I knew there were flexible connectors that could be used to connect to the warm and cold water source. I wondered if they were included with the faucet. Just as that question crossed my mind, a Home Depot employee happened to walk by. I stopped him and asked, "Are those flexible water source connectors included with the faucet?" He grabbed the faucet box, looked it over, and then said, "Absolutely!"

We headed home to begin the installation adventure.

After arriving home, I gathered all the tools necessary to install the faucet. I emptied all the items from under the sink in preparation for my work. I opened the box, removed the contents, and found (perhaps you saw this coming) that there were no flexible connectors! Naturally, I was upset. I decided to try to use the old connectors, which were made of copper, but I bent one during the installation, and I was afraid it was going to leak.

At this point I didn't trust anyone at the Home Depot, but I decided to head back there anyway to get the flexible connectors. I found the connectors in the plumbing aisle; I had brought the old one so I could be sure to purchase the correct length and connection size. I was trying to choose the right connectors by comparing the old with the new, when, lo and behold, the very same employee came walking around the corner. When I explained what had happened, he apologized for his mistake, then asked what I was doing. I told him I needed to know which flexible connectors would fit. He looked at the one I was inspecting. I asked whether it would fit. He said, "Absolutely!"

What do you think I did at that point?

Of course. I looked for a second opinion. I felt I could no longer trust him or his information.

According to Peter Drucker, successful organizations are no longer built on force but on trust. That doesn't mean people must like each other on a social level for the organization to succeed; it does mean, however, that they must be able to count on one another and must be able to create functional, open, honest, and accountable relationships.

It is our duty to do a better job of earning trust than that Home Depot did (at least initially) with me. We owe it to ourselves, to our organizations, and our customers. Why is trust so important? Because we need trust to eliminate unhealthy fear and unhealthy criticism from the workplace.

DEFINING TRUST IN THE WORKPLACE

Shockley-Zalabak, Ellis, and Cesar describe trust as the willingness to be appropriately vulnerable because of the presence of the following five factors:

- Competence of co-workers and leaders.
- Openness and honesty (the amount and sincerity of information).
- Demonstration of concern for employees with empathy and listening, being reliable and dependable in actions.
- The ability to share common objectives, goals, values, and beliefs.
- Reliability and integrity (people doing what they say they will do).

Their research using these five factors has shown a statistically significant connection between trust, job satisfaction, and organizational effectiveness. I have boiled these five factors into four because reliability, integrity, honesty and openness are all so close to being the same concept.

Here then are my own top four characteristics of trust within the organization, drawing on the work above:

- **Integrity, Openness, and Honesty**
- **Demonstration of concern**
- **Shared common objectives or goals**
- **Competence**

All four of these must be managed by a leader!

Now that you know my four elements of workplace trust, let me pose a question. Which of the four elements of trust was missing in the Home Depot employee whom I asked for a second opinion?

Was the missing ingredient the first item on the list: integrity, honesty or openness? No! He clearly had integrity, because he had told the truth as he knew it. If he had lied or purposely misled me, he probably would not have attempted to help me the second time. In fact, if he had no integrity, he probably would have avoided me altogether!

By the way, Warren Bennis points out that integrity is the basis of all trust; he also sites a study that demonstrates an example of how a policy or company standard can encourage behavior that damages trust. In this study with six thousand executives, 70% felt pressure to conform to corporate standards that compromised their own ethics or integrity. An environment that creates pressure to break integrity will damage trust and therefore damage performance. Telling the truth respectfully, being open and honest, and behaving with integrity form the basis for a trusting relationship.

Having eliminated option number one, let's move on to number two on the list. Did the Home Depot employee have concern for me? Yes! I believe he did. Clearly, just as with his integrity, he would have avoided me if he had no concern. He even had expressed his concern by apologizing to me.

How about number three? Did we have the same common objectives? Yes! He wanted me to be able to install the faucet. My ability to have everything I needed to make the installation was necessary for him to make the sale.

In fact, we're looking at a deficit in area number four. It was the employee's competence that was missing. He gave me the wrong information. He was either misinformed or did not have the correct information to share. That's where the trust broke down.

Here's the point: When leaders demonstrate that they trust employees, the result is a significant increase in a demonstration of responsibility, an increase in performance, and an increase in customer service measures. Influencing business outcomes requires trust that is built into the structure and the culture of an organization. Trust must be an integral part of the organization to effectively influence the desired outcomes. The team, the team collaboration, and the individual success all rely on this type of systemic trust.

So: What do you think the Home Depot employee did with the information that he made a mistake?

Whenever I ask this question, I usually hear one of two answers:

"Maybe he tried not to make the same mistake again."

"Maybe shared the mistake with the rest of the team."

My question is this: Is it a success if he simply attempts not to repeat the same error? I believe the answer is no. The reason for that answer lies in the fact that he may be avoiding discussion of mistakes because he fears the consequences of discussing them!

In a very real sense, it is the manager who fails if the team member does not share the mistake, and his response to it, with the rest of the team. If leaders can create a culture of trust, employees will naturally share their mistakes and work as a team to ensure they are not repeated. The typical performance appraisal process prevents this, because people often fear they will be criticized or punished if they tell the truth.

The Home Depot story demonstrated how competence must be managed in order to manage trust. Integrity is another part that must be carefully managed. Integrity means doing what you say you'll do. Integrity also means keeping your word and being congruent in your actions, which of course means simply that what you say and what you do are aligned. As always, actions speak louder than words, so it follows that leaders who exhibit integrity greatly improve their influence with others.

A good example of incongruent leadership is a leader who demands that everyone be respectful of his or her time, and then makes a habit of being late for meetings. Expecting or demanding behavior or courtesy from others, courtesy that we don't ourselves deliver, is one good way to damage our influence.

CINDERELLA MAN

In the 1920s, James J. Braddock from Bergen, NJ, was a powerful professional boxer. A movie entitled *Cinderella Man*, released by Universal Pictures, depicts his story. There is a scene at the heart of the movie that demonstrates Braddock's strength of character, his faith in himself, and his commitment to values. His son had stolen a slab of salami from the butcher shop when no one was watching. At that point, Braddock was out of work, like millions of others were during the Great Depression. His electricity was about to be shut off for non-payment; he had no cash and no food for his two young children; and he was recovering from a serious hand injury that was preventing him from boxing. Braddock came home and discovered what his son had done, then told him it was wrong. He insisted that his son bring the meat back that same day. What a powerful lesson in integrity and honesty!

THE RENTAL CAR

Our trust definition also includes showing concern and/or respect. Here's a true story that illustrates the importance of that principle.

During a recent trip, my wife and I arrived at the San Diego airport in preparation for our trip home to New York. As we turned in our rental car, we were greeted by a young woman who told us her name was Nikki and informed us that there was a great promotion going on if we chose to participate. We could win a free weekly rental or up to $1,000 if we participated in a brief survey about our customer service experience. She explained that she too could win a bonus if we mentioned her name. She repeated her name so many times —Nikki, Nikki, Nikki – that it became very obvious she wanted us to complete a glowing survey about how fantastic her service was. Her concern was clearly about Nikki, and not about us.

A few minutes later we were in the terminal and needed to check in. We chose a self-service kiosk to print our boarding passes. After a few moments the machine froze up and I became frustrated. A customer service person for the airline saw my frustration and approached. She apologized for our inconvenience, rebooted the machine and swiftly, without being asked, completed our transaction, printing both boarding passes. She then handed me coupons good for a free cocktail, which could be redeemed on our flight.

Which customer service person managed trust by showing concern? Clearly, the second incident demonstrated significant concern for both our business and our personal well being. That built up trust.

SHARED OBJECTIVES

Another area for creating optimum trust is aligning on shared objectives. A leader who is able to align his/her team on a clear strategy built on shared objectives will create trust; one who doesn't present such a strategy will not.

Employees need to see how their jobs align with the strategy of the organization. A leader who can communicate a clear strategy and then orchestrate the communication of that strategy for every employee will be able to accomplish remarkable results. The trust created when the entire organization is aligned on shared objectives will propel the organization forward in a dramatic and powerful way. Here's a real-life example of that.

One early morning I traveled to what I thought was going to be a networking meeting at a diner near my home. That meeting turned out to be a bust because I had gotten the date wrong; no one showed up. I reminded myself that a mistake can often turn into a blessing, and decided to buy myself breakfast. In the middle of an excellent omelet, I decided I needed more coffee. I placed my cup on the edge of the counter in hopes that my waitress would interpret my subtle message when she passed by. Within a few short moments a hand grabbed my cup and I heard, "More coffee sir?" I looked up and said, "Yes please!" I then noticed that the young woman asking me this question was *not* my waitress.

I wondered: "Why would a waitress other than my own, want to serve me more coffee?" It was then that I realized that I was receiving EXCELLENT "teamwork" service!

When it came time to pay I gave at least a 50% higher tip than usual. I had received exceptional service from a team that was aligned on the objective of providing excellent customer service. Their willingness to share responsibility to ensure my satisfaction sent me a clear message of trust and alignment. Since that day, I have been on the lookout for more opportunities to visit that diner!

TRUST AND WELL-BEING

One significant benefit of high levels of trust is a sense of well-being. A recent study explored the link between performance and employee well being, and concluded specifically that the management behaviors consistent with developing trust and support made a significant positive difference in the well-being of employees. On a similar note, the International Association of Business Communicators conducted a study that clearly demonstrated a connection between trust and performance. Their work shows how organizations with high levels of trust can expect to experience:

- Measurable economic performance
- Increased cooperation
- Reduced opportunistic behavior
- Increased participation, reduced crisis
- Conflict that is productive (not destructive)
- Improved adaptability (handle change)
- Decreased transaction costs
- Reduced litigation costs
- Reduced unnecessary bureaucratic control
- Reduced administrative expenditures
- Increased information flow
- Improved relationships with supervisors

The Ritz-Carlton® leadership philosophy sums it up nicely. It explains that true leadership responsibility is the process of building a trusting environment .... so leaders and followers can feel free to participate fully in accomplishing mutually valued goals with processes that are predictable.

THE ENEMY OF TRUST

If trust is what makes a workplace function optimally – and it is – then performance appraisals are the enemy of trust.

Even when the employer's stated intention is a positive one, – say, improving motivation and performance —employees often end up feeling unfairly rated and unfairly judged. This sense of being judged reduces trust. Any reduction in trust damages creativity, fun, and productivity and therefore creates just the opposite of what the employer hoped to accomplish. Even if just a few employees have a negative experience during the performance appraisal meetings, the word can spread to the entire population, causing an increase in fear: "I might be next."

Here are five unintended negative outcomes of conducting performance appraisals. Trying to improve the individual parts of a system, without changing the system itself, will inevitably create these effects!

1. First and foremost, trust is damaged. As we have seen, trust is a vital ingredient in high performance organizations. Since nearly 80% of employees feel that they are among the top 25% within their group, any rating below that will cause disappointment and damage motivation and trust. The use of appraisals in an organization suggests an automatic lack of trust. When managers believe they need to use appraisals, they also tend to believe they need to grade, rank or bribe employees to do get them to work. This assumed lack of trust by management will generally create a similar response from employees.

2. Relationships suffer. Once trust is damaged, the relationship is damaged. An appraisal, by definition, places one person as the judge and the other person as the "defendant." A critical element of any open and honest relationship is respect, yet the appraisal typically increases the probability that one of the parties (usually the employee) will feel disrespected, because

judging employees instead of evaluating workflow methods feels both unfair and disrespectful to the employee.

3. The customer comes last. Employees concerned about a certain rating (especially one tied to compensation) will likely put their own welfare ahead of others in hope of attaining the desired rating. Often, this means compromising the customer's welfare.

4. Root causes go undetected. The circumstances that actually affect employee performance are important and difficult to evaluate. "Stuff" happens prior to a performance appraisal that can positively or negatively impact an individual's performance. For example, a report may have been submitted late because accurate information took more time to collect than anyone anticipated. How can a manager rate an individual poorly when performance is impacted by such circumstances?

5. Overall performance suffers. Employees fear damage to their reputation, loss of credibility and embarrassment; low ratings may affect their employability, their relationships, and their ability to advance. Employees who fear a low rating will take fewer risks and suggest fewer new ideas.

Table 1

The "Old Way" – Command and Control	The "New Way" – Systems Thinking
1. Improving individual performance improves organizational performance	1. Improving processes improves performance
2. Evaluating employees improves employee performance	2. Evaluating employees most often destroys motivation, commitment and risk taking
3. Managers are able to fairly and accurately evaluate employees separate from "system"	3. It is impossible to remove bias, favoritism or stereotyping from the appraisal process
4. Pay-for-performance will improve organizational performance	4. Pay-for-performance creates unintended consequences

Once organizations begin to recognize the ineffectiveness and damaging effects of their appraisal system, they can embark on fixing it. Usually the "fixing" focuses on one of two areas: (1) improving the design of the process (e.g. new criteria, new scales, more interaction, more raters, and more frequent appraisals) or (2) improving the implementation (e.g., better training, stricter rules to ensure timely execution, checking raters for consistency and bias tendencies). These improvement initiatives accomplish little, however, because the problem with appraisal is neither in the design nor in the implementation. The underlying assumptions —the basic premises and beliefs upon which the appraisals are built —are what are flawed. Unless the underlying assumptions change, there is no hope for any performance appraisal process to deliver predictable positive results!

JIFFY LUBE® AND THE LAW OF UNINTENDED CONSEQUENCES

Years ago, I used to go to Jiffy Lube® all the time. I like to take care of my car; I'm particular about getting the oil changed on time. I'm an ideal customer for a company like Jiffy Lube. One day I was at Jiffy Lube and the manager walked up and said, "Mr. Hauck, you need a new PCV valve." I said, 'What's that?' He explained that a PCV valve is a component that helps with emissions and told me that I really needed to replace it.

I said, "Well wait a minute. I just had the car at the dealer and they inspect everything. Are you sure I need that?" He said, "Oh, absolutely; look how dirty this one is." And he rubbed his thumb across it, then showed me his thumb. It was covered with black sludge.

I said, "Okay, how much is it?"

It cost fifteen bucks. I told him to go ahead and put it in.

Half an hour later, I was at the cash register; my car was ready. I handed the manager my credit card and I looked above the cash register on the wall. I saw a whiteboard that read GOALS FOR THE WEEK. Beneath it, there were sales goals: so many for oil changes; so many for air filters, so many for (you guessed it) PCV valves.

I said to the manager, "Wow, that's interesting, the goals for the week. Where do you get those?" He said, "We get them from the home office; they fax them down to us every week on Monday and we work to meet them between Monday through Saturday."

I asked, "Do you get paid a bonus on those?" He said, 'Oh, sure. I get a bonus and the guys out in the shop get a bonus too." I said, "That's interesting. How are you doing this week?" He said, "You know, not too bad. We are a little behind on PCV valves, but we're catching up." I later learned that many Jiffy Lube customers had placed complaints on-line about unnecessary PCV valve replacement.

How much business do you think I give Jiffy Lube now?

Pay for performance combined with a Performance Appraisal can create unintended consequences. The two can tend to create an environment with a focus on what is perceived as best for the employee ... and not so much what is perceived as good for the CUSTOMER. We can see that syndrome play out over and over again in other organizations. What appears to be short-term gain ends up costing the organization dearly in the long run.

CATASTROPHIC COSTS

In June 2001, fifteen of the nineteen September 11 terrorists obtained visas to enter the United States, They got those visas in Saudi Arabia.

According to experts familiar with the visa issuance process, *none* of the visas should have been issued because of clear red flags that appeared during the process. The experts don't hold the consular officers accountable, because they were taking their lead from the supervisor who created an environment of courtesy for Saudis. The experts fault the policies and guidelines within which the officers were forced. As a combined result of direct encouragement of their supervisor, fear of criticism of their work, and a threat of withholding of bonuses, officers purposely ignored red flags that would have prevented all of the fifteen of these hijackers from legally entering our country. The standing law (#214-b) was purposely violated, in accordance with the supervisor's wishes.

The consul in question refused fewer than 2 percent of Saudi visas, whereas the worldwide refusal rate for temporary visas was approximately 25%. According to some experts, if the law had been followed, the attack on the US could perhaps have been averted.

PUTTING IT ALL TOGETHER

Without a systems approach the following results are often seen:

- Blaming the person and ignoring the influence on that person by the process (e.g., blaming the Dunkin' Donuts employee for the sugar).

- Blame creates anxiety, which stops creative problem solving and innovation.

- The focus is on the person, not the process. Being angry at the employee takes the focus off the real root cause and prevents us from identifying real solutions.

- There are unintended negative consequences. Employees looking for extra compensation, approval, or a good rating in their performance appraisal may hide mistakes, often with a supervisor's connivance.

- People may also withhold information from coworkers to compete for (for instance) bonuses or perks.

EMBRACING SYSTEMS THINKING

Unfortunately, systems thinking is a rare commodity in most organizations, because it is not taught in our schools.

CEOs who do not embrace systems thinking usually create fear. Fear is persistent in organizations when employees and managers both assume the other is solely focused on their own personal self-interest ... and/or when there is the perception that one person's success is at the expense of the other's success (a zero sum game). Any policy or procedure that reinforces this assumption will be a barrier to trust.

On the other hand, when fear is reduced and trust is increased, employees will naturally become more committed to their work, to their organization, and to delivering value to their customers. Trust is the opposite of fear and is a critical element of every interaction in an organization. It creates the foundation for quality, performance, and profit. Like any foundation, if it is solid, it allows the organization to grow with confidence and consistency. Any policy or process that may undermine this foundation must be changed. The point must be repeated: *The typical Performance Appraisal is just such a policy!*

A WORKING WORLD BEYOND FEAR

Dr. W. Edwards Deming wrote at length about the need for the transformation of the organization. His method, "Profound Knowledge and the Fourteen Points", is a method for transformation with which all executives should be familiar. Very few organizations have had enough discipline to implement all fourteen points. Most of the few that try to implement improvement efforts end up implementing only a few of Deming's points.

One of the most important points discussed by Dr. Deming is number eight: *Drive out fear.* This brings us once again to the issue of trust. Deming writes: "No one can put forth his best performance unless he feels secure ... secure means without fear, not afraid to express ideas, not afraid to ask questions." Yet 89% of all business organizations in the United States use a formal performance evaluations tool. In addition, 85% of those organizations continue to tie compensation to performance. These are policies specifically condemned by Deming – as deadly diseases.

Driving out fear must be one of the first steps in the transformation of any organization, and the personal transformation of the leader is required first to accomplish this point. Without this personal transformation to a new way of thinking, the same employee behaviors and the same results will persist in the workplace!

"Personal transformation requires a deep understanding of systems thinking. It requires acceptance of the philosophy of win, win," Latzko and Sanders observed in 1993. "Once transformed, one may thereon work toward transformation of his own organization." This is the key action needed to achieve transformation, and the key action required for the creation of trust. The ability of management to see how their own behavior can be a barrier to the organizational improvement they seek will enable the organization to enhance trust and move toward transformation. Managers are very often unaware, however, how rare trust is in their own workplaces.

The opposite of trust is fear, and fear is still the tool by which too many managers manage. Fear will invite the probability of incorrect figures or cheating. In order to make (achieve the) unrealistic goals set by management, employees may tend to manipulate numbers or results. All too often, the policies and demands of management encourage employees to break integrity to meet objectives. On this subject, Deming writes: "Fear invites wrong figures. Bearers of bad news fare badly. To keep his job, anyone may present to his boss only good news."

What is needed is trust in staff and management alike. Without trust the truth becomes dangerous – or at least elusive. As Ryan and Oestreich observed: "At least 70 percent of the 260 people we interviewed said that they had hesitated to speak up because they feared some type of repercussion." If this is still the environment in which we and our people are operating, we must not delude ourselves that the transformation Deming advocates has taken place. It hasn't!

What is needed to accomplish this transformation? Leadership! Deming writes: "As I use the term here, the job of a leader is to accomplish transformation of his organization. He possesses knowledge, personality and persuasive power."

What is needed from leaders is a level of trust that provides a blanket of security for employees during change efforts – a level of trust that makes the often stressful and confusing process of change possible. Without that trust, transformation is impossible. Yet instilling it in the workforce is one of the steps executives most commonly ignore.

Driving fear out of the workplace is essential; tools that enable managers to transform their own thinking and behaviors first is the best way to create hope for improvement in this area.

Managers must not merely *say* that they trust employees, but must provide tangible evidence that they believe, and act on the belief, that employees can be trusted. The crucial step in this area is obvious: we must eliminate damaging policies such as performance management and pay for performance.

Trust implies freedom. When you trust people you can let them be free to make decisions on their own without strict supervision and control. An increase in trust creates the "free of fear" environment we seek. An increase in trust will render performance management and pay for performance policies unnecessary.

The four-part definition of trust that I am proposing in this book, namely...

Integrity, Openness, and Honesty

Demonstration of concern

Shared common objectives or goals

Competence

... is, I believe, completely compatible with Dr. W. Edwards Deming's famous Fourteen Points of Management, which are reproduced below.

Deming's 14 Points of Management

Shared Common Objectives

1. Create constancy of purpose towards improvement.» In other words, replace short-term reaction with long-term planning.

2. Adopt the new philosophy.» The implication is that management should actually adopt its own stated philosophies, rather than merely expect the workforce to do so.

Improving Competence

3. Cease dependence on inspection.» If variation is reduced and

therefore quality is improved, inspection becomes less necessary. Random inspection to measure the quality level is acceptable to maintain quality.

4. Move towards a single supplier for any one item.» Multiple suppliers means increased variation between lots.

5. Improve constantly and forever.» Constantly strive to reduce variation.

6. Institute training on the job.» If people are inadequately trained, they will not use the same best practices, and this will introduce variation.

7. Institute leadership.» Deming makes a distinction between leadership and mere supervision. The latter is quota- and target-based.

Integrity and Concern

8. Drive out fear.» Deming sees management by fear as counterproductive in the long term, because it prevents workers from acting in the organization's best interests.

9. Break down barriers between departments.» Another idea central to Total Quality Management is the concept of the "internal customer," the notion that each department serves not the management, but the other departments that use its outputs.

10. Eliminate slogans.» No, you shouldn't post this sentence in your cubicle. The idea here is that it's not people who make most mistakes - it's the process within which they are working.

Harassing the workforce with slogans without improving the processes is counter-productive.

11. Eliminate management by objectives.» Deming saw production targets as encouraging the delivery of poor-quality goods. He was right, but decades later, we're still fixated on numerical targets.

12. Remove barriers to pride of workmanship.» Many of the problems outlined in this book reduce worker satisfaction and pride.

13. Institute education and self-improvement.» Deming was committed to ongoing growth.

14. The transformation is everyone's job.» This is – or at least should be – self-evident.

Reprinted with the permission of MIT Press.

Dr. Deming's Fourteen Points are, first and foremost, prescriptions for high levels of trust. In them, he describes a different way of thinking about an organization and about leadership. He proposes that management focus on the context of the organization and the systems within the organization rather than on trying to improve each individual employee. Specifically, he writes: "A basic principle here is that no one should be blamed or penalized for performance that he cannot govern. Violation of this principle will only lead to frustration and dissatisfaction with the job, and lower production." (Deming, 1986, *Out of the Crisis*, page 251).

To recap: Managers need to spend less time managing individuals and more time managing the organizational environment or its context. The context of an organization can be defined as the environment created by the culture. Organizational culture comprises the attitudes, values, beliefs, norms and customs of an organization. The context for work is created by senior leaders and will either discourage or encourage specific attitudes, and behaviors – and will always have a dramatic effect on results and the bottom line.

As Deming wrote: "In place of judgment of people, ranking them, putting them into slots (outstanding, excellent, on down to unsatisfactory), the aim should be to help people optimize the system so that everybody will gain."

Deming's insights, taken together with the other concepts you've learned in this book, can create an effective context for an effective organizational development program. Why? the focus is on system performance, not on individual performance.

A HUMAN RESOURCE CHALLENGE

What are some of the most important challenges facing Human Resource Managers today? A recent article in Industry Week Magazine points to a serious problem: civility in the workplace. Industry Week reports:

"In a study by Christine Pearson, research professor of management at the University of North Carolina's Kenan-Fagler Business

School, 100% of the people surveyed said that they felt they had been treated rudely, disrespectfully, or insensitively by a co-worker."

Pearson's study also indicated that 53% of those surveyed said they had lost work time worrying about past or future confrontations with fellow employees. What's more:

- 37% said such incidents caused them to reduce their commitment to the organization
- 28% said they lost work time avoiding the other person(s); and
- 22% decreased their effort at work.

In summary, the major issues facing Human Resource Professionals today are human issues. Experts in Human Resources are struggling to find better ways to improve staff morale, reduce destructive conflict and improve the overall civility of the organization. In a word, we need an increase in TRUST.

Trust is the real key to improved performance.

A recent study by the Mercer Organization pointed to improved communication as the key to workplace productivity and employee loyalty. Through its 2002 People at Work Survey, Mercer surveyed a sample of 2,600 US workers about their attitudes and perceptions regarding their job and organization. 8% of the questions in the 180-question survey related to workplace communication. The findings show:

- Employees want more information to help them do their jobs
- Among employees who rated their organization good at keeping employees informed, only 6% said they were dissatisfied

with the organization.

- On the other hand, among those who rated the organization poor at communication, 39% said they were dissatisfied.

High levels of trust and an effective communication process are keys to improving the workplace and addressing the major issues of civility, conflict and morale. The Values and System Management Model provides that method.

The need for trust, especially while conducting a performance appraisal, is reinforced by other research. In 2008, 376 leaders who graduated from a Connecticut Chamber of Commerce leadership training program were surveyed about their impressions of the performance appraisal process. 74 participants ended up answering the survey questions. These participants were from 35 different organizations. All of these organizations conducted performance appraisals with a rating or grade. In addition, 80% of the participants had employees reporting to them and 80% tied compensation decisions to the appraisal results. Furthermore, 47% of participants were at the senior leader position in their organization.

The results demonstrated how the Performance Appraisal is very weak on delivery of its promise to improve performance and it fails miserably when trust between the supervisor and employee is absent. For example, only a little more than half of the participants (54%) said the appraisal process improves organizational performance. In other words, 46% said it either made things worse or had no impact at all. Furthermore, less than half (47%) said it improved individual performance.

Participants with high trust in their supervisor (a trust rating of 6 to 10 on a ten point scale where 10 is high and 1 is low) said the appraisal improved organizational performance 73.5% of the time whereas participants with low trust said it helped only 12.5% of the time.

According to the same survey, participants with low trust said their individual performance was improved only 20% of the time. Fully 80% of participants with low trust of their supervisor said the appraisal process either damaged their individual performance or it had no impact at all. Furthermore, participants with high trust of their supervisors and senior leaders said the appraisal improved their individual performance 70% of the time.

In short, *trust matters* when assessing performance. This confirms the need to manage the trust and relationship between the leader and the employee *before* beginning any performance discussions and *before* any recommendations for performance improvement.

Epilogue:

The Three Key Takeaways

We have discussed three basic principles of leadership. Let's look at them once again.

Principle #1: It's the leader's job to create the most useful context or environment.

Principle #2: The way leaders think determines environment, which in turn determines organizational behavior. The Values and System Model described in this book is the most useful paradigm for solving problems — especially people problems.

Principle #3: A leader must consciously and continuously manage trust with all constituents.

If I were challenged to combine these three into a single sentence, the sentence might sound like this.

The way leaders think about people and problems will inevitably determine the behavior of the leader and influence the behavior of employees therefore, people's performance is only as good as the system within which they perform and that in turn is only as good as the thinking of the leader.

Aligning the Team

A laser beam can cut through steel. Its intense focus of energy is an effective tool for medical and industrial applications. Diffused light is useful but focused light transforms.

What if a leader could take the diffused energy of a group of people and create a focused team capable of "cutting through" any difficult problem with minimal wasted time?

This is the power of alignment. The ability to align a team of people will be the next major competitive advantage for leaders to develop. The companion volume to this book, *Aligning the Team*, provides both the philosophy and the process to create a sustainable team environment.

The four elements of trust that must be managed are competence, integrity, concern/respect, and shared objectives. A leader must know how to manage each of these areas well. The next book, ***Aligning the Team,*** provides the HOW. To learn more about *Aligning the Team,* please e-mail me at *Wally@WallyHauck.com.*

ABOUT
WALLY HAUCK

ally Hauck is a source for employee engagement solutions. Wally helps leaders to bring out the best in people. Organizational problems often appear, on the surface, to be "people problems", when in fact, the real problems are actually the organization's underlying broken internal systems. Relationships, trust and loyalty are more important now than ever before because the real value of an organization lies in the minds of the employees and their ability to solve problems.

Wally is a Certified Speaking Professional or CSP. The Certified Speaking Professional (CSP) designation, established in 1980, is the speaking industry>s international measure of professional platform skill. CSP is conferred throughout the International Federation for Professional Speakers only on those who have earned it by meeting strict criteria.

Wally has a Bachelor of Arts degree in Philosophy from the University of Pennsylvania; an MBA in Finance from Iona College; and earned his PhD in Organizational Leadership from Warren National University in 2008. His book **Blueprint for Success** provides ideas that can help leaders unlock their potential, remove metal blocks to success, and provide new insights to accelerate positive change. Wally's chapter, The Power of Influence: 7 Secrets for Successful Leadership, provides leaders with insights to create an environment of trust, continuous learning, and employee loyalty. Wally has worked with dozens of firms and government agencies in the last decade.

In addition:

- President National Speaker's Association Connecticut Chapter 2008-2009
- Past President of American Society for Training and Development (ASTD), Fairfield County CT Chapter
- Past Member of the Board of Directors of the Bridgeport Chamber of Commerce
- Past Member of the Board of Directors for Bridgeport Rotary
- Past Board Member for Literacy Volunteers of America
- Speaker for The American Society of Quality at national conventions
- Speaker for The International W. EDWARDS DEMING INSTITUTE
- THE NINTH ANNUAL RESEARCH SEMINAR and

Author for the Research Paper: "THE WHITE FLAG®: a Predictable Method to Build a Culture of Trust and Accountability."

- Speaker for the W. Edwards Deming Institute Annual Conference
- Co-developed an alternative Performance Appraisal called the Complete Performance Improvement Process (CPIP). This tool enables leaders and employees to manage trust and improve their competencies while improving organizational performance.

Please access the web site for further in formation: www.wally-hauck.com

Optimum Leadership
167 Cherry Street #404
Milford, CT 06460
203-874-8484
www.wallyhauck.com

15707817R00059

Made in the USA
Charleston, SC
16 November 2012